Fueled:

Business Strategies to Grow and Influence Your Next Steps

Kimberly DeShields-Spencer

Fueled:
Business Strategies to Grow and Influence Your Next Steps

Fueled:
Business Strategies to Grow and Influence Your Next Steps

1. Business 2. Marketing

ISBN-10: 1981316639
ISBN-13: 978-1981316632

Thank you...

Charles for always being supportive, loving, and caring. You are always there to ensure nothing stops me from pursuing my dreams. Thank you for always being there for me. I love you beyond words and I am so proud to be your wife!

Christian and Cayden, you are my heart. You both are my reason why I do what I do each day. I could not ask for better sons. I love you both more than I can ever say.

Mom and Dad, your endless support means more to me than I can ever express. Truly you both are the BEST parents God has blessed me with. You both taught me what truly matters in life and that has helped me become who I am today. I love you both immensely.

To my clients, you truly matter to me. I am so blessed to know each of you and I love being on this journey with you. Thank you for trusting me to walk alongside you in building your dreams.

Areas Covered

Seek to be worth knowing, rather than being well known.

If you are anything like the clients I work with, you are committed to your business, you are focused on getting results, and you really want to build a business that blesses you and your family.

This book is a compilation of the top blogs I have written over the years on topics such as: branding, marketing, profit development, client engagement, and how to define your position in your market. They are written to guide you through the process of how to really design your business brand to be clear, marketable, and profitable.

I want you to read this book and walk away with:

- A clear understanding of how to position the value you offer to your clients
- Clarity in how to develop an engaging brand
- How to cultivate systems in your business
- How to gauge whether what you are communicating is being translated
- An understanding of what to track in your business
- Plus, so much more!

To Your Impact and Success,
Kimberly DeShields-Spencer
Founder, UImpact

How to Reposition Yourself

What I notice often is many entrepreneurs simply state what goals they want to accomplish, and then place deadlines next to each goal to stay accountable. So, what is wrong with that? Plenty!

What is often lacking in accomplishing your goals is how you strategize in positioning your planning to execute them.

Standard Goal: "I want to increase my network, so I will attend at least 4 new networking groups each month."

Here is this goal written in a way that positions you. "I want to increase my network, so I will contact the meeting planners of 4 groups I want to connect with. I will then ask them how I can become one of their speakers for their monthly events. I plan to do this each Monday of this month until I have booked 4 opportunities to present."

Now, you are positioning yourself in front of your target audience. Instead of meeting a couple of people, the whole room will be listening to and learning from you-and will want to meet you afterward. Those same people will visit your social media links while you are speaking. Additionally, they will be visiting your website to learn more about you. Now, you have increased the number of potential connections by simply moving from attending an event to speaking at the event.

Standard Goal: "I want to make five thousand dollars a month in my business." I hear this one often.

Position this goal differently. Look at the activities you are focusing on each month. Do they position you to reach this monetary goal? Are your activities generating income? It is not enough to *say* you want five thousand dollars, you must position your activities to reflect that.

PAUSE. REVIEW. IMPLEMENT.

What goals do you plan to accomplish in the next 90 days? Plan to be productive – not busy.

I believe in writing out your goals so you can clearly see what you are striving for.

Take each goal and outline clearly what steps you will take to achieve it.

_____

_____

_____

Two Systems You Need to Generate Client Leads

You do not know how long a customer has been considering whether they want to work with you. Oftentimes, we don't see the other products, services, programs, and so forth that potential customers are considering before they choose to work with you.

Realize that no matter what you sell: insurance, makeup, t-shirts, financial services, furniture, food, pet products-whatever-everything has an incubation period. That means, to win the business of and truly convert a prospect to a buyer (and a buyer to a loyal fan), it's your job to get in front of (and *stay* in front of) your prospect.

This also means that you can't expect a prospect to immediately convert to a customer. Therefore, you need to constantly generate leads and help lead them through the gestation period to convert them into a fully mature, raving fan.

Two Systems to Master in Your Business:

1. Create marketing and sales systems. Putting systems in place ensures you are regularly attracting and leading prospects to your product or service, and engaging with them to help guide and sell to them during that gestation period.

- How often are you marketing?

- How often are you tracking your results?

- What strategies/tools have you used that are most effective?

- Do you have a marketing calendar? (Do you follow it?)

- Do you have marketing sequences in place that run automatically?

2. Create systems for **every stage** your prospect, client, customer, or patient will go through. For example, you can create a system to attract new clients, to follow-up on potential clients, to manage current clients, to educate prospects and clients, and to help customers use your product or service.

3. Having systems in place means you won't have to chase after clients, customers, or patients-nor are you losing sales because you didn't have time or forgot to follow up with them. Don't worry about having a perfect system. You don't need the perfect system to get started. Put something in place, then tweak as you go.

Without systems in place, prospects, customers, clients, and patients will never find out about you, or they will fall through the cracks causing lost revenue, or worse. This will keep you in feast-and-famine mode!

You'll be more efficient, more productive, and convert more prospects into paying customers. Plus, by ensuring consistent contact with your prospects, customers, patients, or clients, you'll always have a steady flow of new business.

PAUSE. REVIEW. IMPLEMENT.

When it comes to creating or revamping systems, it is best to start with the one that causes the most impact in your business.

What is one system that you need to review or revamp? Write out what your current system is so you can see what is needed and not needed.

_____

_____

_____

_____

The Way You Make Me Feel...

Someone once said, "People won't remember what you said, but they will remember how you made them feel." This is the core of an influential personal and business brand. To make a true impact and resonate strongly with your target audience, you've got to make an emotional connection. Fifty percent of every buying decision is driven by emotion. Emotions shape the attitudes that drive decisions and behavior.

The most powerful question you can ask yourself is, "How do I want people to FEEL when they experience my brand?"

As you are asking yourself that question, I want you to also take the time and ask yourself the following:

- Do people connect with the information I am sharing?
- How am I getting to know my audience as people and not just potential clients?
- How is my client care engagement process?
- What would my clients (past and current) say about their experience with me?

How do you Build and Strengthen these Connections?

Look Under the Hood: Examine your processes, procedures, and even the messages you send to your clients. Where is the focus? Is it on you, or your clients?

Every time you serve your clients, ask; "If I were them in this situation, how would this experience feel for me? Did working with them feel simple and easy? Did my issue get resolved quickly? Consistently examining your processes helps to illuminate areas of strengths and opportunities for growth.

Plug In: Make a point to regularly listen to your clients. Listen for validation or inconsistencies with your brand image. Do you regularly listen and respond to your clients? Do you truly understand their concerns and needs? What's beneath the surface? Listening can be a challenge, because it means you must be open to hearing what your clients like and dislike that define their perceptions of your brand.

PAUSE. REVIEW. IMPLEMENT.

How you make your clients feel shapes their experience with you.

What are some ways that you feel you connect the most with your clients? What do you feel you need to work on to enhance their experience?

_____

_____

_____

_____

Out with the Old, In with the New

I am not sure about you, but I love to look at processes and freshen them up. It is so easy to get stuck in utilizing the same systems, same programs, and the same approaches. For example, the SWOT Analysis (Strengths, Weakness, Opportunities, and Threats) is a great framework, but I have learned that when you use the same approach each time, you tend to lose a sense of creativity in how you map out your next steps. Truth is, you already know your strengths, weaknesses, opportunities, and threats.

Let's reframe how you can look at your strengths, weaknesses, opportunities, and threats from a branding and marketing perspective.

Review each of the six core areas below and look at them with new eyes.

- **Obstacles** – In examining your current positioning in your market, what are the most serious obstacles that you face in growing and leveraging your brand?

- **Objectives** – What are your most significant and/or challenging goals and areas of focus?

- **Occurrences** – What events took place during the period you're evaluating to shape future opportunities and threats?

- **Ordinary** – What are some programs, services, or products that you have had for some time that you can refresh or create an updated version of? What are some thought processes that have kept you stuck in your comfort zone you need to identify-and then break out of that place?

- **Obsolete** – What processes, relationships, clients, things, or ideas are no longer in alignment with your brand's strategic plan? Also, what is no longer relevant now as you explore your future situations?

- **Organization** – Where is your business today as it relates to what you outlined in your goals? Have you made your milestones mark? Have you increased your revenue? Have you increased your visibility? Examine where you are in your business.

PAUSE. REVIEW. IMPLEMENT.

Walk through each of the six core areas I mentioned and ask yourself the questions that I posed. Jot down your thoughts below.

_____

_____

_____

_____

_____

Developing Your Creative Capital: Using a Banana and an Orange

When I hear someone say they are not creative, I immediately want to show them that we all have a sense of creativity in us. I truly believe that we each have various outlets that our creativity flows into. You may struggle in finding creativity as it relates to your business, however, when you tap into what you are creative in, you can translate that to your brand. You may be great at scrapbooking, creating new basketball plays, painting, coming up with new recipes, and the list can go on.

Thinking creatively is a state of mind that enables you to approach tasks, problems, and situations with openness.

Let's look at a banana:

When was the last time you ate a banana from the wrong end? Probably never, because no matter how hard you try to peel a banana from the stem, you can't. I tried just to see if it was possible. As I thought about how that can relate to branding, I had an "aha" moment. Some of your best ideas come from thinking about your brand, your clients, and your services in a completely new and non-traditional way. When you need to generate fresh ideas, look at everything you offer and your solutions from a creative approach.

Can you add new elements to how you approach a situation? Can you reframe solutions for your clients?

One of the greatest things I do to grow is learn from other industries. Why? It provides a fresh perspective on how I can approach solutions. Consider getting inspiration from new sources.

Peel back all the layers you can to a solution and seek new perspectives. Write down all the layers you can, and don't worry about what is wrong or right about what you write down. Just write, and then sift through the solutions that best fit your audience.

Let's look at an orange:

When was the last time you were able to peel an orange in one swift move? Like the banana, you probably haven't done that. With an orange, you have to keep peeling off the skin in small chunks which causes you to pause and focus on the action of peeling back the skin. So, how does this relate to your business?

There are two things peeling an orange can do to help facilitate the creative process:

First, look at how you are disseminating information to your clients and in your marketing. Are you offering step-by-step solutions or small, bite-sized value nuggets that they can implement immediately?

Second, it gives you the **Power of the Pause**. We tend to operate our businesses at lightning speed and often don't pause long enough to allow innovation to take place. It is a struggle to be creative when you are constantly operating at high speed. **Enjoy more moments of pause so that you can look at things from a relaxed frame of mind.**

Remember: Thinking creatively is a state of mind that enables you to approach tasks, problems, and situations with openness.

PAUSE. REVIEW. IMPLEMENT.

There is such value in taking the time to really pause when it comes to working on your business.

Take a minute and ask yourself: How effective is my marketing? Do I need to re-vamp my approach? Do I need to re-vamp my target audience? Write down what comes to mind first when you read these questions.

_____

_____

_____

Be anything but predictable.

Standing Out:
The Blue Box

It represents high value and exceptional quality luxury. When someone receives this blue box they instantly feel valued by the one giving them this box.

Tiffany blue box was first introduced in 1837. The color known as Tiffany Blue was selected by founder Charles Lewis Tiffany for the cover of Blue Book, Tiffany's annual collection of beautifully handcrafted jewels, first published in 1845. Tiffany Blue is also referred to as robin's-egg blue or forget-me-not blue, this distinguishing color may have been chosen because of the popularity of the turquoise gemstone in 19th-century jewelry.

It is amazing that he realized early on the importance of brand positioning at a time when few people thought about such things. He determined blue that would be associated with Tiffany and introduced the box, knowing that he could differentiate gifts from his store that were presented in the distinctive box. To this day, the blue box is one of the most coveted and most protected brand attributes of Tiffany. Without the box, the value of the contents reduces instantly. With the box, it becomes a true piece of differentiated luxury.

Tiffany's classic Pantone No. 187, Blue Box demonstrates that a brand can maintain its relevance in a competitive market over more than 150 years by being consistent in its brand attributes and associations. Tiffany retains a differentiation strategy of highly perceived value--incremental costs of their jewelry might not be that much higher than competitors, but the perceived worth to customers is much higher and they are willing to pay more to get a Tiffany item.

One would argue that there is stronger quality jewelry than Tiffany's. That may very well be the case. However, the brand has been positioned so strongly in the market that people focus on the perceived value of Tiffany's versus the actual value of the jewelry the box contains.

This brings me to you.

- Does your brand standout?
- Does it have a strong point of differentiation?
- Is your name synonymous with what you specialize in?
- What does your audience think about when they hear your name or the name of your company?

Let's go one step further. Developing a strong brand is more than creating what makes you different. Your brand needs to be consistent all around. Whether I go to your website, social media outlets, blog, or attend your event, I should clearly see consistency across your brand.

How can you create brand differentiation?

- **Through Your Story**. While some people's journeys are like yours, no one has walked in your shoes. Your story or stories gives you a distinct value differentiator.

- **Through Your Style**. One element we forget in business is to have fun. While some information is the same, how you choose to deliver it can set you apart. Remember, there are seven different learning styles that you can appeal to. Explore, have fun, and deliver information in your style.

- **Through Your Stance**. You make the choice on how to enter your industry. Too often, we don't really craft how we want to roll out our brand and message to our audience. Make an impression that causes your audience to want to get to know you more. How do you do this? By simply being *you*-infused into your brand.

PAUSE. REVIEW. IMPLEMENT.

Your turn. Take some time and answer these questions:

Does your brand standout?
Does it have a strong point of differentiation?
Is your name synonymous with what you specialize in?
What does your audience think about when they hear your name or the name of your company?

_____

_____

_____

Be so good they can't
ignore you.

Four Types of Content That Generate Results

If you are like me, you know that content marketing is crucial to the success of your business.

The entire purpose of content marketing is to establish yourself in your market, connect with your audience, and drive more sales to your business. For your content marketing to be effective, it must be rooted in consistency and in the following key areas.

Let's delve into four types of content areas:

- **Interest Me**: I speak often about creating that emotional connection with your audience. The truth is, they want to feel some connection to you and your business. The more connected they are, the more likely they are to share your content purposely. The more your content is shared, the further your reach. An example of this can be your marketing videos, which are designed to create interest. People must be intrigued by what you have to offer. If they are not intrigued, they generally won't move forward in reaching out to you.

- **Inform Me**: Your content should teach or equip your audience in some fashion. We live in a day and age where people are researching more before they make a buying decision. If you and your company is researched, what will they learn about you? Will they find useful articles, blogs, tools, and content? Will they see how knowledgeable you are? The more someone understands the features and benefits of your programs and services, the higher the likelihood they will purchase.

- **Influence Me**: What does your content influence your audience to do? Do you want them to call you? Do you want them to register online? Your content should trigger your audience to act. I'm a firm believer that content should be brand-focused and -driven. By this I mean that what you create should be driven by what you want your clients to achieve. Review your content and ask yourself whether you are influencing your audience.

- **Convert Me:** Let's all be honest. We are in business to grow our business, which means attracting new clients. Structuring your content so you are addressing their questions and objections places you in a great position. When they contact you, they will be in a place of "yes."

PAUSE. REVIEW. IMPLEMENT.

When it comes to staying relevant, your content is what will keep your audience plugged into you.

Go back through the four areas: Interest Me, Inform Me, Influence Me, and Convert Me.

Below, jot down how you can challenge yourself in the four areas I outlined.

_____

_____

_____

Do You Allow This to Hinder You?

As a strategist, I find that it is often not the lack of skills or talents that prevent someone from growing their business. The issues are embedded in the mindset and perceptions that you have as an entrepreneur. It is so crucial that you recognize what may be hindering you from really and truly exploding in your business. Let's delve into four of those mindsets now:

1. **Lack of Belief Mindset**: Not really believing that you have the skill sets to be an amazing entrepreneur. Not trusting your own instincts or your natural God-given talents. Not really believing that it is possible to have all that you desire.

2. **Acceptance/Value Mindset**: This one is huge. If you don't value what you bring to the table, it will be hard to convince someone else to value your expertise and your offerings. Create value in your time, in how you work with clients, in your personal growth, and value that saying no is a good thing…as is saying yes to areas that stretch you.

3. **Complaining Mindset:** Complaining about all the resources you don't have versus focusing on the ones that you do have, or finding ways to get the resources that you need. Complaining about the lack of clients rather than figuring out how to gain new clients.

4. **Blame Game Mindset**: Have you noticed that people still blame the economy on why things are not moving in their business? Also, blaming other people-past and present-for why you are not moving forward in your business. Those are easy scapegoats. You have to look at what you are doing to move your business forward. Look at how you are showing up every day.

PAUSE. REVIEW. IMPLEMENT.

The battlefield of the mindset is one of the hardest battles to fight-especially as a business owner.

Which of the mindset obstacles listed do you need to address and why? What do you plan to commit to doing in addressing it?

_____

_____

_____

_____

The Number One Reason That Your Marketing May Be "Missing the Mark"

Lack of clarity. That is the simplest way I can state this. Lack of clarity in your marketing, in how you position yourself in your market, in your messaging, and in your brand overall can cause your ideal clients to be confused and uninterested in what you have to offer. This all leads to you feeling frustrated, because your activities are not yielding the desired results you planned for.

I've learned that an important part of having clarity in your brand and messaging lies in knowing who you are, and knowing who you are not.

You see, the core purpose of marketing is to elicit a response from those you are targeting. If your marketing is not generating the response you desire look at your messaging, activities and how you are positioning your brand.

Let's look at a couple of examples

Example 1: If people view your marketing materials and still ask you many questions to gain a better understanding of what you do and offer, that is a sign that your marketing is NOT clear. However, this does not mean they are not interested. The key here is to structure your marketing content so that you are addressing their questions and objections. Why? So that when they contact you they are in a place of "yes," and not in a place of "lack of clarity."

Example 2: If you are attending several networking functions a week, contacting those you connected with, and are not getting a response, consider evaluating how you articulate what you do. Are you sharing too much, or too little? Are you clearly stating what you do in a differentiated way? Are you trying to connect, or trying to sell?

On a personal note, the clearer I became about my brand and its messaging, the more confident I became in sharing what I do. The more confident I became, the more comfortable I became in communicating the value and expertise that I have in this. The result was I attracted clients who felt safe and confident in working with me.

PAUSE. REVIEW. IMPLEMENT.

One of the best ways you can challenge yourself is to test whether your marketing is conveying the right message.

Make a list of everyone you can ask to review the entry points into your business (for example: blogs, websites, social media). Ask them what they feel your business is conveying. This will help you know if your marketing is clear.

_____

_____

_____

Lessons from *Do Us a Flavor*

Have you ever tried the following chip flavors?

- Cheddar Bacon Mac & Cheese
- Cappuccino
- Wavy Mango Salsa
- Kettle Cooked Wasabi Ginger
- Cheesy Garlic Bread
- Chicken & Waffles
- Sriracha

Some sound yummy, and others...well, I will let you be the judge of them. Each of these flavors are a part of Lay's Chips' annual contest called Do Us a Flavor. Last year, it was between Cheesy Garlic Bread, Chicken & Waffles, and Sriracha. This campaign went viral and truly engaged a national audience in a fun contest over these flavors. I must admit, I did jump in and try them all...and I voted.

Lay's is such a great example of Creativity and Engagement.

Lay's has been one of the top-selling snacks in America for more than 75 years. As with any company, they were looking for new ways to engage their audience with the increase of competition in their industry and ever-evolving technology. Thus, was born the Do Us a Flavor campaign.

Now, let's look at your business and see how we can apply what Lay's has done to your level of creativity and engagement.

- Are there any programs, services, or events you host that could use a makeover, reinvention, or addition? Can you add a new program? Can you add a creative element? Can you add more engagement?
  (Ex: Lays designed its annual Do Us a Flavor campaign. This promotional event infused new customers, created new awareness of the brand, and engaged the company's existing customers.)

- Are you finding new ways to engage your audience with your current offerings? Do you get them involved in your process (outside of a survey)? Do you create intrigue for them to want to learn more?
  (Ex: Lay's designed a national content on customer-created flavors. The company has used social media, celebrity endorsements, creative TV commercials, etc.)

Remember, there is so much "noise" competing for the attention of your clients' ears. Find ways to keep your brand fresh, cutting-edge, forward-thinking, creative, and engaged with your audience.

PAUSE. REVIEW. IMPLEMENT.

This is the fun part: finding new ways to engage your audience. Keeping things fresh, current, new, and engaging keeps people plugged into you.

What are some creative ways you can enhance how you engage your audience?

_____

_____

_____

_____

What Promise Are You Making?

What do all these brands and their slogans have in common?

1. M&Ms – "Melts in your mouth, not in your hands."

2. Hallmark – "When you care enough to send the very best."

3. Red Cross – "The greatest tragedy is indifference."

4. Nikon – "At the heart of the image."

5. Harley Davidson – "American by Birth. Rebel by Choice."

6. Disneyland – "The happiest place on earth."

7. Ajax – "Stronger than dirt."

8. Kodak – "Share moments. Share life."

Answer: Each of these slogans conveys a promise to you as a potential client or consumer. Look at each slogan, and then think about the company it represents. You will see that the slogans align with what their company represents.

Does your business slogan or tagline align with your brand promise? Is it catchy and memorable? Does it conjure up positive imagery and connection to your business? For example, Nike's "Just Do It" tagline immediately makes you think of Michael Jordan, the swoosh symbol, or some form of sports. Those three words, "Just Do It," connect you to their brand.

Slogans reinforce your brand identity and the reputation of what your business stands for. For example, my tagline is "Where entrepreneurs play big and thrive." So, when I work with someone, they are expecting to thrive in their growth in their business and income. They are expecting to step out of their comfort zone and "play big." That is my brand commitment to my audience. This must be reinforced in our entire marketing and branding strategy. If you have a great slogan/tagline that conveys your brand promise, good for you! If you don't and you are not sure if it is necessary, please take this into consideration: when you have a slogan attached to your business, it occupies the best real estate there is for an entrepreneur-in your potential clients' subconscious. This will cause them to recall your business when it comes to making buying decisions.

If you find that you are not sure how to develop a slogan/tagline, always go back to what you want your clients and potential clients to think and feel about your business. Review your attributes and always connect it to your "why."-why you started this business, and why this "promise" signifies your commitment to them.

PAUSE. REVIEW. IMPLEMENT.

In business, keeping your word means everything. What your business communicates speaks volumes. What promise does your business make?

Now ask your clients and anyone associated with your company whether they feel you deliver on that promise.

_____

_____

_____

Keeping Up with the Joneses

We all know the Joneses. They are the people who seem to have it all. They have great homes, take the most amazing vacations, are always impeccably and fashionably dressed, and seem to have the life that so many want.

They are also the people who leave others around them wondering, "Why can't I have that life?"

But the Joneses have one major problem.

What could it possibly be? Their problem is that all too often, what you see with them is not real. They are so busy trying to be who they are not that they often lose themselves in the pursuit of getting, obtaining more, and creating perceptions of status.

This shows up very often in business today in the forms of:

- Striving to be like those whom you admire in your industry. Instead of looking at what someone is doing and seeing how to make it your own, what happens is the focus becomes doing exactly what they do.

- Spending money on activities that you presently may not be able to afford.

- Presenting something to your ideal audience that is not rooted in who you really are.

I am a firm believer that we each have so much to bring to the table. So instead of copying or taking what is not ours, we should look at how we can make something better, more creative, and more engaging for our audiences. Standing in your brilliance is the best way to stand.

PAUSE. REVIEW. IMPLEMENT.

List ten ways you bring value to your clients.

Once you do this, review whether you clearly articulate the ways you bring value throughout your branding and marketing.

_____

_____

_____

_____

Warning Signs That Your Brand Is Dying

Have you ever been in a position where you try to warn someone that they are headed in the wrong direction, but they refuse to listen to you? Worse yet, they refuse to see the warning signs? It is hard to witness when those blaring warning signs are ignored by someone. I want to outline some warning signs as to why your brand may not be growing in the way that you had hoped.

This list is great for you even if your brand *is* growing. Why? It allows you to see trouble-before it comes.

- **Let's Make a Deal**: You're constantly being asked to discount your prices, and you feel you have no option but to do so.

  A Suggestion to Avoid This: People love to price shop, however, when you really communicate your value and address all their objections (before they state them) in your marketing copy, you reduce attracting price shoppers.

- **Trying to Catch Their Attention**: You keep changing your "story" to fit your latest product launch, campaign, or new advertisement.

  A Suggestion to Avoid This: Select one or two stories that unify your brand message and product offerings.

- **No Diversity**: You only offer one product or product line and it does not allow you to diversify.

  A Suggestion to Avoid This: Sometimes, when you experience impressive results with a program or product, you tend to want to stay with just that same program/product. Offer at least three programs that are in alignment with your business, so you provide options for your clients.

- **Over-Growing**: You keep developing and adding new products, services, programs, and campaigns with the expectation that sales will catch up at some point, however they have not.

  A Suggestion to Avoid This: Build smart. Before adding new offerings, survey your clients, look at the current buying trends in your market, assess whether what you are offering is in line with their needs and if it is being offered at the right time.

- **Overdoing It**: Your brand architecture is confusing to your customers – too many product names, sub-brands, logos, taglines, etc., fighting for attention and market share.

  A Suggestion to Avoid This: Reduce the brand clutter. If it's not memorable, they will not remember you. A confused buyer does not buy, refer, or connect to you.

- **Lack of Consistency**: There's no consistency in your process of marketing, in your messaging, customer experiences, or your brand's touch points (which we will cover soon.)

A Suggestion to Avoid This: Develop a system you know you can follow for all your processes. Systems help your business flow better, and help to gain/retain the trust of your clients.

Look for these warning signs so you can avoid the death of your brand.

PAUSE. REVIEW. IMPLEMENT.

Regardless of where you are in your business, examining what is or isn't working is always important.

Review the warning signs I listed and ask yourself whether any of them connect with you. If so, jot down what you would like to do differently.

_____

_____

_____

It's not who you are that
holds you back.
It's who you think you're
not.

Branding Touch Points

I wanted to provide you with a great checklist that you can use to evaluate where you are currently in building your business brand.

An effective brand allows people to get to know who you are, and it positions the core of your business. It creates a personal, responsive (emotional) connection to you.

Understanding and formulating your brand is the foundation and heart of your business. Before marketing, before networking, before jumping out there (or restarting), branding should be at the core.

Here are some questions you can ask:

- When you look at all the entry points into your business, is your brand message consistent and clear?

- Does your brand create an emotional connection with your audience? Does it compel them to want to get to know you or stay connected to you?

- Are you clear on what your brand is and the message you want to convey?

- Are the attributes of your brand clear throughout your business?

- Are you attracting the clients, partners, joint venture relationships, and opportunities that you would like?

- Are you offering "today's" solutions for your clients? Do you have a finger on the pulse of what they need and want today?

- Do you find ways to know what is currently going on in your industry, so you can offer relevant and timely solutions to your clients?

- Are you clear on what your unique selling position is?

- Have you mapped out what your client's experience looks like when working with you from beginning to end?

- Are your service offerings, products, marketing implementation plans, and programs consistent with your brand?

- How often do you conduct a personal marketing and brand audit on whether your messaging, activities, and desired results are aligned with your brand goals?

This is a great checklist to review to see how you are shaping and cultivating your business brand.

PAUSE. REVIEW. IMPLEMENT.

Looking at touch points is something I love to dive into when reviewing what my brand is communicating.

I would like to challenge you to answer at least three of the questions I poised.

_____

_____

_____

_____

Doing This Can Cause You to Lose Clients Fast

There is one simple thing that can cause you to lose potential clients fast. Once you have lost them due to this, it is virtually impossible to ever get them back.

You can also lose your current clients with this one simple thing. Not only will it cause your clients to stop using your services, but they will not refer anyone to you. That is the power of this one simple thing.

This one simple thing is *not keeping your word.* It's saying you'll do something, and then not doing it. Suppose you say to a potential client, "I will send you that additional information tomorrow." Then tomorrow comes, you get busy, and you don't send it until the day after. *No big deal* you think to yourself as it's only one day late and it's not going to make a significant difference. Yes, it probably does not make a difference to the potential client whether they get it tomorrow or the day after. However, if you don't do it when you said you would, it will make a HUGE difference in what the client thinks of you.

What do you think a potential client would think of you if you said you would do something, no matter how minor, and you did not do it? They could possibly think:

- This person is unreliable. I can't trust them.

- This person lacks integrity.

- I can't trust this person to do what they say they will do.

- If they are not keeping their word on these simple things, can I trust what they are saying about their service?

- If this is how they treat me before I become a client, then how will they treat me when I do?

- I am obviously not that important to them.

Suppose a current client calls you with a problem, and you promise to call them back with a solution later that day. You get busy on another project, and forget to call. What do you think they might say to themselves about you? They could possibly say:

- This person is unreliable and lacks integrity.

- Now that I am a client, they obviously care less about me.

- I am not going to buy any more services if this is how I'll be treated.

- Is there someone else I can find to do this for me who is reliable?

- I am not going to refer anyone to them and risk my reputation.

So, keeping your word is important-not only in gaining new clients, but also in keeping your current clients and gaining referrals.

Keeping your word is also important for how *you* think about you. If you don't keep your word, you take a hit on your own confidence and self-esteem. You start to lose trust in yourself. This impacts all areas of your business and personal life.

When you have said you will do something by a certain date, and something comes up that prevents you from doing it, simply communicate and renegotiate as soon as possible. Communicate with the client, apologize, and get their confirmation that it is okay if you now complete it by date "x" instead.

Starting today, I urge you to honor your word with everyone-no matter how small or insignificant what you have committed to appears to be. Then, observe how clients react, and how you feel. Client attraction will be just one of the rewards. Let me know how it goes.

PAUSE. REVIEW. IMPLEMENT.

I cannot stress enough how vital keeping your word is as a business owner. This is an area I see people struggle in.

If this is an area you struggle with, jot down what you want to commit to doing when it comes to keeping your word. Will you give yourself more time to complete a task? Will you set up reminders for the deadlines you have? Will you arrive fifteen minutes early for appointments?

_____

_____

One Day or Day One
You Decide

What You Track, Grows!

One of the questions I am always asked by a new client is: What numbers should I be paying attention to? Great question, isn't it? I simply say, "You will want to keep track of all the numbers that you would like to grow, and it is imperative that you keep a handle on your expenses." There is a great saying that goes: *what you don't track does not grow.* Tracking numbers is one activity I have seen many entrepreneurs fail to do, and it costs them more in time, money, and resources when they are not tracking what is taking place in their business.

Below are some suggested areas where tracking your numbers can help you gauge the health of your business:

- How many clients do you have in each program, or in general?
- How many referrals are coming in each month?
- How many products have you sold?
- How many people are visiting and clicking though the pages of your website?
- How many chargebacks or returns did you have?
- How many customer leads are converting to clients?
- What expenses are going out each month?
- How much income is coming in daily?
- How many newsletter sign-ups do you have each month?
- How many people are actually opening your newsletter?

- How much is your social media reach growing daily/weekly/monthly?

Tracking your business growth on a daily, weekly, and monthly schedule will aid you in developing a sustainable and profitable business. Anytime someone asks you about your business and its growth, you should clearly know what is going on daily.

Taking the time to really understand what your business numbers are saying will:

- Assist you in determining what marketing campaigns will work best and when.

- Enable you to estimate the best places to set your marketing information.

- Enable you to determine what your clients' buying trends are throughout the year.

- Enable you to determine which content your subscribers respond to best.

This is honestly a very brief list of the many benefits that tracking your numbers will provide for you. You will become much more empowered to really understand how to position your company for exponential growth.

So, the main question is: *How* do you track this information? Simply put, whether you work best with spreadsheets or accounting software, develop a system in which by the end of each day, week, and month, you are reviewing the items I previously outlined for you.

If you want your business income to grow, then track it. If you want to reach more clients, track those numbers. If you want all your expenses to increase, then track them. Remember, what you track will grow. Wishing you the best in tracking your growth to greater success!

PAUSE. REVIEW. IMPLEMENT

What you don't track will not grow. I stress tracking numbers faithfully with every client I have. Through tracking, you will see the health of your business.

What are you currently tracking? What do you need to start tracking?

There are no shortcuts to any place worth going.

Prioritizing Your Day
(What to Start With?)

This is not about managing your time, because I don't believe you can manage time-you can manage what you *do* with your time. This is about focusing on the right activities that will help you accomplish maximum results with your business.

This is a topic that, so many are constantly struggling with. However, it is one that you can easily overcome and manage.

There are three areas that I would suggest you start with.

- **Focus on Your Clients/Members** – One of the first things I suggest doing each day is focus on the activities that generate your income. This can include client meetings, projects, client calls, consulting, networking, etc. Oftentimes, you can get "busy" responding to emails and calls that have nothing to do with your clients. They are the reason you have a business, so it is imperative that you focus on what they hired you to do.

- **Focus on Marketing Development & Strategy** – I suggest you spend an average of four hours a day on marketing. Why? You need to keep the flow of clients coming in to sustain a business. Focusing on marketing can include email marketing, product launches, networking, meeting with potential joint venture partners, and setting up potential client meetings.

- **Focus on Your Money Flow** – What you don't track, you won't grow. If you are not tracking the flow of your revenue, income, and debts, then you won't know the true health of your business.

While there are many aspects of your business you should pay attention to, I would suggest that these three are areas that you should focus on especially.

PAUSE. REVIEW. IMPLEMENT

What you focus on tends to grow. I shared about focusing on your clients/members, your marketing, and your money flow.

What do you need to focus on and why? What do you plan to do differently in this area?

_____

_____

_____

_____

Are You Awakening the Senses?

If you can't tell by now (though I hope that you do), I love to create new and fun ways to engage my audience. Business should be fun and engaging. The more you keep things exciting, the more engaged you and your audience will be as well.

So today I want us to explore how to engage the senses to draw in your audience. I am talking about sight, sounds, taste, touch, and smell. The formal name for using the various senses in your marketing is called Sensory Branding. You can use one or multiple senses to engage your audience.

Let's explore the five areas:

- **Sight:** This is the most targeted of the senses in marketing, because it generates the greatest response from your audience. You know immediately at the first view of a website, logo, marketing material, presentation, etc. whether you are drawn in or intrigued by the brand or the person behind it. Fashion retailer Gina Tricot says: "the eyes buy 70 to 80 percent of what people buy." That is why how you choose to visually represent your business is vitally important in helping you position yourself.

- **Sound:** "Do the Shopping Cart," Staples' break-out commercial that was designed to draw parents to their stores, is a great use of sound. This commercial took on a life of its own and influenced greater customer engagement and buying trends since they launched it. You can probably think of several companies that are infusing music into their marketing to connect their audience with their brand.

Music can effectively influence your clients' buying behaviors and connection to your business, events, products, etc. That is why it is a great idea to use music at your events and in videos where applicable. Music unites and connects people. So, ask yourself how you can introduce sound in your business.

- **Touch:** Using this sense is another way to strengthen the brand connection. It links the image and experience together. Touch can be infused by the materials you use; comfort of the product and weight are other factors. Touch is now being applied to emotional connections as well.

- **Smell:** It may surprise some, but the sense of smell is used in branding because it increases the customers' remembrance of the brand. This sense is most linked to our emotional recollection and connection to the experience that we have. It can create instant connections between a brand and other memories. For example, one thing I do is have special fragrant candles in the rooms I host events in. People always remember the smells when they walk in. When they remember that scent, they think about the event they attended.

- **Taste:** This sense is closely tied to food and beverage industries. When you look at shows like Top Chef, you can see how each chef has their own distinct way of cooking. The judges always knew the chefs by the taste of their food and the style in which they prepared it. When you can remember a special dish or drink, it will connect you to where you were at that time. This can also work well with events that you host. People remember the details of what you feed them as well.

When you use the senses in developing your marketing think about your audience and what you want them to experience. Keep in mind that you should have fun with this. Use the senses to draw in your clients.

PAUSE. REVIEW. IMPLEMENT

This may be a stretch when trying to see how you can incorporate any of the senses into your marketing. But I know you can do it.

Select one the senses I mentioned and write what you can do with it when it comes to your marketing or branding. There is no right or wrong response.

_____

_____

_____

You are exactly where
you need to be.
Trust the timing of your
life.

Are You Making These Mistakes When Branding Yourself as a Speaker?

I spent eight years running my own professional speaker management agency where we marketed professional speakers and handled all aspects of their businesses. I gained a vast amount of experience and knowledge in what meeting planners really look for- which is why I know there are many myths and outdated teachings, so many speakers are following.

I want to help you identify some of the most prevalent ones, so you can debunk them and start working towards adding speaking into your business.

1. **"I am not a speaker."** HUGE myth. If you love what you do, you will naturally want to speak about it. You *should* speak about it. What you should determine is what type of speaker you are. There are twelve various categories you can be in, and here are some of them: Keynoter, Workshop Speaker, Trainer, and Retreat-Style Speaker. Knowing the type of speaker you are greatly shapes your approach to incorporating speaking into your business.

If you don't love the big stage, that is fine. You can speak to your audience through your own programs, or you can speak to audiences outside your company. Remember, people want to see you, get to know you, hear what you have to say, and connect with you.

Through speaking, you can connect with your audience ten times faster than through a website or newsletter. Speaking builds your credibility factor with your audience.

2. **Signature Talk**. Don't waste a lot of energy on developing a signature talk. Focus on a signature focal point for all your talks. Whether you speak for marketing reasons or as a professional speaker, select your focal points. If you have one main talk that you market all the time, then you will be boxed in with that topic only. You limit your marketability. Focus on creating two to three titles around the focal point of your expertise. This gives you more leverage and room to scale the speaking aspect of your business.

3. **One Sheets.** You don't need a one sheet. Yes, you are reading this right. Meeting planners do not look at one sheets, and this has been statistically proven. They are more focused on your speaking videos and overall branding. So, if you are stressing about having the perfect one sheet, or preparing to have one created, I would encourage you to reconsider that decision. Invest in great videos that highlight snippets of your talk.

Focus on:

1. **Incorporating some form of speaking into your business.** Your voice matters, and your audience needs to hear it. This can be through teleseminars, hosting your own events, speaking professionally, holding your own webinars, etc.

2. **Determining your focal point.** Think about what you want your name to be synonymous with. What do you want to be known as in your market?

3. **Getting experience**. Whether you speak only to your peeps, or you want to speak professionally, get experience. This is not about being a perfect speaker. It is about being comfortable with what you have to share.

PAUSE. REVIEW. IMPLEMENT

Now that you have thought through a few areas, what do you plan to do?

Pull out your calendar. Put what you write below on your calendar so that you have a date for when you will complete that action item.

_____

_____

_____

Don't force pieces that don't fit.

Before You Reap a Harvest, Cultivate This...

Here is a great saying by Henry Ford: "Before everything else, getting ready is the secret of success." As a matter of principle, preparation is the most essential element of achieving success. While that is not a big secret, I am still fascinated by the number of entrepreneurs who do not plan intentionally and strategically for where they want to go. Your harvest in business is highly dependent on the quality and quantity of the seeds that you cultivate. Different crops require different cultivation.

Cultivate the Core: Without a focused and healthy intention for pursuing your business goals, you will end up becoming a prisoner of your own dreams. Really understanding the *core reason* of why you are launching that new program or service, why you are creating a membership program, and why are you entering into a joint venture relationship fuels every action you take. However, you must cultivate how you will stay tied to the core reason of your why. Why? Because it is too easy to lose your "why," your "core" in the details of the activities it takes to develop your business. When you lose your core, it will be evident in what you attract.

Cultivate Your View: While I love vision boards and setting goals, the key to really implementing what you want to see happen is rooted in how you see yourself. If you are developing content rich programs, but you inwardly believe that no one is going to buy them or work with you, you will attract what you think.

You must cultivate how you view:

- Yourself personally
- The definition of success
- Yourself as the expert in what you do
- How you view who you are meant to be

If your view is distorted, then how you walk the path towards your goals will be murky and clouded at best. You need to have a sense of true clarity in what lies ahead of you.

Cultivate Your Marketing: It is not enough to say, "Next week, I am going to 'XYZ' for my business." The most successful companies and entrepreneurs spend time outlining their marketing and how they will position their services, launches, and products at least six to nine months out. Ask yourself the below questions, and then map out the details:

- What / When / How is your pre-enrollment process?
- What / When / How is your post enrolment process?
- What experience is your audience having?
- What marketing tools am I going to use and when will I be integrating them?
- How am I going to measure my company's marketing?

Cultivate your core, your view, and your marketing-and those three components will help you cultivate a harvest for your business.

PAUSE. REVIEW. IMPLEMENT

Before you can cultivate anything, you must cultivate your view: how you view yourself, how you view success, and why you are building your business.

Take a minute to write down how you see yourself as an entrepreneur, how you define the type of success you want, and finally, why you are building your business.

_____

_____

_____

Two Branding Rules You Should Break

I have always believed that how I represent my business is a true reflection of who I am as a person. To represent what I do in the truest sense of the word, I had to determine what my approach to client solutions would be, how I would cultivate client relationships, how I would design my marketing materials, and how I would brand my company. Taking the time to determine these areas allowed me to represent who I was. I did this by not following the rules.

What I see often is entrepreneurs get lost in defining how to incorporate their style, their client solutions, and their own special touch in representing their business.

So, I say get away from some of the "this is how you should do it" type of thinking and teaching. You stand out best when your own unique thumbprint is represented. Here are two rules that I feel you should break to really help you stand out in your own way.

Break the "This is What They Do" Rule: What I hear way too often is: "This is how it is done in the industry." If you are following the pack, then how can you place yourself in a position to lead? Pay attention to the trends, and then create your own trend or enhance a current trend. If you are calling yourself an expert or an authority in a field, then ensure that you are knowledgeable of what is going on, and then put your spin on the solutions. Just because something has been done a certain way for a long time does not mean you have to keep doing it the same way.

Break the "I Have to Use These Colors/Look/Style" Rule: As an entrepreneur, you are encouraged to stand out, identify your differentiators, highlight your unique selling propositions, and the list goes on. However, so many entrepreneurs box themselves into branding that does not represent them.

I love the colors red, black, and orange. So, when it came time to design my website and marketing materials, I decided to go bold and use red and orange throughout all our marketing. Was I told that would be too much? Yes! Was I told to use more professional colors? Yes! However, those colors represented me and who I am.

That is all I am trying to convey. You do need to be professional, but don't sacrifice your personal style or your unique look. Use what represents you.

PAUSE. REVIEW. IMPLEMENT

I am all about breaking the rules that keep you inside a tight box. As a business owner, you must be open to new things and opportunities.

Write out the top three solutions you provide for your audience. Once you do that, review which one you can offer a new approach to. Think about what others are doing and how you can offer a slightly different approach.

_____

_____

_____

Your Best Branding Tool is Right Under Your Nose

We have all heard it said that branding is not about your logo, website, font size, etc. This is true. It is not about any of those things. However, those components do shape the perception of your brand. The reality is, your brand is rooted in your business identity. It is what you are known for in your industry, in the eyes of your clients, and what people think when they hear your name.

Here is an example: When people hear the word "Apple," most immediately think about computers. The positioning of their brand is so strong that their logo, website, and colors come to mind immediately. Their reputation and quality of their products quickly comes to mind. Even Steve Jobs comes to mind when people think about Apple.

This leads me to ask you: What comes to mind when your audience thinks about you? What builds your brand reputation? The tool that helps you truly answer each of these questions with unwavering confidence is right under your nose: your tongue.

The fact is, what you communicate to others and what others communicate about you to their communities shapes your brand.

What you communicate:

- Can change people's perceptions of you and your business for either good or bad.

- Can attract or repel your client base from wanting to connect with you.

- Can create or destroy opportunities for you.

- Can either help you build your income or reduce it.

- Can also cause you to stand out or blend in with everyone else.

It doesn't matter how much money you spend in branding your business, in networking, in designing your marketing materials-and the list can go on. What matters is *how*.

Ask yourself what do people think and feel when they hear your name.

- Are they influenced by you?

- Do they think about the quality of what you offer?

- Are they encouraged by you and what you offer?

- Are they compelled to take action?

- Do they immediately know what you do?

- Are they clear on the solutions that you offer?

If you are unsure about what you feel you are communicating and what is actually being communicated, try any of these suggestions:

- Identify eight to ten people that make up your community, and design a one to three question survey that asks on-target questions about the perception of your brand. *(Your community can be made up of current clients, past clients, your team, colleagues that you trust, a sampling of your online audience, and even the vendors that you work with.)*

- Find out what people type in when searching your company. There are many analytic tools available where you can input your company's name and see what keywords are associated with your brand. This can be a very telling exercise.

PAUSE. REVIEW. IMPLEMENT

I find that what we feel we are communicating is often not being received in the way we think.

What comes to mind when your audience thinks about you? What builds your brand reputation?

The best way to answer these questions is to poll your audience. Ask them, and write down what they say.

_____

_____

_____

Don't lose yourself in the temporary.

It is All in the Follow-Up

I wanted to share a very important habit of truly successful entrepreneurs. This is a habit that you should introduce into your relationships with potential and current clients. I am sharing this because I have realized that one of the most critical skills that entrepreneurs lack is not following up or following through. It is not just about "leaving money on the table." When you don't follow up or follow through with clients, potential clients, or on your word, you can hurt your brand reputation.

If someone sends you an email or leaves a voice message, it is crucial that you respond as quickly as possible.

Responding through email is very easy; there is no excuse for not replying to an email. But even if a phone call is necessary, you still must follow up in a timely fashion.

As you are building your business, you should want and expect clients to respond to your emails, calls, and proposals; however, you must ask yourself if you do the same to others. It is just good business to always give people the respect of a response.

There is a saying that goes: "Fortune is in the follow-up." That statement is so true! If you don't have a consistent follow-up system in place, you will leave potential business on the table. I see this all the time, and I really don't want that to happen to you.

Three Key Issues:

If you hear "no," "not now," or "not at this time," typically, you won't circle back and check in with the client to see if the situation has changed. The same holds true if you don't hear any response from anyone.

Here is what usually occurs: You share your information at an event, or directly with a client. They sign up on your website or through a contact card to stay in touch. Yet, there is no consistent flow of communication (newsletter, email, direct mail). You have no clear follow-up system in place.

- When you meet someone at an event, what do you do?
- How often do you follow up with a potential client?
- What methods do you use for following up?
- After a client has completed a program, what happens next?
- If they have purchased a service, what happens next?

Start asking yourself these questions.

Here are three suggestions on how you can follow up more effectively and consistently:

Just Checking – Contact someone within twenty-four to forty-eight hours after meeting him/her at an event. However, if for some reason they choose not to move forward with you in that season, follow-up with them sixty to ninety days later. I call this my "Just Checking" phone call or email. You never know whether someone's situation has changed, and they are ready to work with you. So, I would call them and just let them know that I'm "just checking" on them and wanted to see if things have changed.

Handwritten Note Card – I love the personal touch; people like to feel special. Sending a handwritten or personal note can make a significant difference in connecting with your potential client. Going that extra step really shows that you care. Ask yourself when was the last time that you hand wrote a note to a client, new partner, vendor, or even a friend.

Consistent Contact – Follow-up is not just a phone call or email. Following up also comes in the form of how consistent you are in your marketing (such as your newsletter, direct mailing, etc.). Create a system for how often you will send out your marketing tools to stay in touch with your existing and potential clients.

PAUSE. REVIEW. IMPLEMENT

One of the most crucial skills that should be mastered as an entrepreneur is how you follow up. It is in the follow-up whether someone decides they want to work with you or not.

What is working and not working for you? What areas do you need to improve in when it comes to your following-up process?

_____

_____

_____

Don't stumble over something behind you.

Your Value, Your Fees

I am amazed by the number of entrepreneurs I meet who do not realize the value of the services they provide and hence are charging far less than they would like to or deserve. Sometimes, this is due to necessity, and in other cases, abject fear of having the confidence to ask for what you want. Your relationship with money hinges on how you will set your rates. I would like to take a moment to see if any of these are true for you:

- You set your fees based on what your competitors are doing, and what you feel the client can afford to pay.

- You set your fees low because you want to get your "foot in the door" and build up a track record of your services.

- You are very good at what you do, but when it comes to sitting in front of a client, you do not ask the right questions.

- The client has received outstanding results from your work, but you have already quoted a set fee and the value they have gained is much greater than what you have earned.

If any of these resonate with you, then read on as this may be of interest and give you a personal breakthrough. The truth is, your value is based on how you see yourself and how you have *presented* that value. The problem isn't only helping the client to understand the value of what you are providing, but more importantly, convincing yourself that you are worth it.

This leads us to: How do I establish value in terms of the buyer's needs? Here are some suggestions:

- **Set an intention** to build a trusting relationship with your prospective client by really working at understanding their needs. Ask a lot of questions at the outset, and don't be afraid to go back to get clarification.

- **Resist the urge to offer solutions** immediately to the client when you begin discussing their problems.

- **Outline clear objectives** of what is required (i.e. increase in sales), and ensure that you are *both* clear about them.

- **Be honest.** Tell the prospect what the options are for your services or products, any quantity discounts you offer, and how payment is delivered. Practice saying this repeatedly until the words and phrases slip comfortably from your mouth.

- **Act confidently** when delivering your fees. Don't downplay your fees. State your fees, and stand by them. Don't make excuses for your fees or ramble on about them.

- **Don't automatically offer discounts**. This tells the prospect that your fees are negotiable. Instead, state your fees and options, then ask them which package is right for them.

PAUSE. REVIEW. IMPLEMENT

One thing I do not like to see is a business owner who does not value themselves through their fees.

Take a minute and write down all the ways you bring value to your clients. Don't edit yourself, freely write all that comes to mind. Then review whether these same values show up in your marketing.

_____

_____

_____

_____

The Final Two Minutes in Your Business

I used to play basketball in high school, and I absolutely love the sport. (I think my husband would say I am obsessed with the game!) What I enjoy is the intensity and commitment that each player brings when they hit that court. I enjoy how each player has a role to play, and when they play together, remarkable results happen.

When watching the NBA finals, I notice that my family and friends sit on the edge of their seats during the 4th quarter, especially for the last two minutes of the game. That is when the players go into another dimension. Regardless of how exhausted those players are, they play full-out until that final second ends and the buzzer goes off. No matter what obstacles the opponent tries to put in place, the other team plays very hard to reach that basket.

That is what you must do in your business. I see some entrepreneurs give up before that final second ends.

They don't see the results they expected, so they give up. They are not getting enough registrants for their workshop, so they give up. They are not getting as many clients, so they give up. They have tried everything, and nothing is working, so they give up.

A true champion in business knows and understands how you start and finish the game.

Let's look at some examples you may relate to:

Game One:

You are hosting your own workshop. Your goal was to have twenty-five people, and only seven registered. You have nine days left before your event. You decide to cancel the event because you don't feel like you have enough people attending, and you don't want to be embarrassed.

- **Your Final Two Minutes:** Instead of quitting and not hosting the event, keep making calls, networking, and reaching out to those who expressed interest, but have not registered yet. You keep pushing and coming up with creative ways to attract the number of people you are looking for. Regardless whether one shows up or twenty-five, you still host your event. You never know who that one person is or knows.

Game Two:

You attend several networking events. You have quite a few hot leads, and you are excited about the potential of having new clients. You go home and call every single person, and not one person returns your calls. You don't want to seem like you're stalking them, and you decide that maybe they are not interested, so you do not reach out anymore.

- **Your Final Two Minutes:** Just because someone does not return your call does not mean they are not interested. As you know, life events can happen to us all. Instead of discarding those leads, reach out to them again one to two weeks later to see if they still have an interest. Keep networking and generating new leads.

Game Three:

You goal for this month is to make $5,000, and you only have two weeks left, and no new leads. So far, you've only generated $2,000. You resign yourself to thinking that there is no way to make an additional $3,000 this month.

- **Your Final Two Minutes:** Ok, so you have no leads, and no idea how to make any additional income. You have fourteen days left in the month. You can go back through older leads to see if there is new interest, create an information product, and schedule a high content/high quality teleseminar. The bottom line is you work as hard as you can with integrity until that final buzzer goes off.

Make those final two minutes count!

PAUSE. REVIEW. IMPLEMENT.

There are times as an entrepreneur when you will feel like giving up. You will feel like you have done all you can do. But it is in those times that you can't stop or give up.

What is your final two minutes? What do you need to do to push toward your goal?

_____

_____

_____

If you can't change the circumstances, change your perspective.

Develop Content That Attracts and Converts

When developing content marketing for your services, you need to focus on:

- Clearly stating the benefits to your clients/customers
- Clearly stating the value that others have experienced with you and your services
- Building the trust that they need to have with you

The main question that you will be answering in your content marketing is: "Why you?"

First: The best content creators see their stories as the keystone of their communications. They don't view content as a task or a campaign. They view content as something rich with possibilities in the way we communicate with clients so that they recognize us before and over any other brand. That sounds easy enough, but it's a huge mental shift for most entrepreneurs.

- **Here's a good test**: Look at what you are sharing with your clients/potential clients. Are you sharing your why? Are you sharing your story? Are you sharing why you started your business? What it means to you? Have you built that connection? Do you feel your clients get a good sense of who you are?

Second: The best content creators have a distinct voice. They have developed a point of view that's unique to their brand and unshackled from "everyday" speak.

- **Here's a good test**: If you mask the visual branding on your content, would you recognize that content's voice as your own? Do you sound and look like everyone else in your industry? If you answer yes, create a list of what you feel you bring to the table that is unique, then use that in your content.

Third: The best content creators take risks. They experiment. And they sometimes fail. As Hugh Macleod says, "We were all given the same box of crayons in kindergarten," yet somewhere along the line, many of us convince ourselves that we're not creative, particularly in a business context. That sort of thinking limits our full potential as people, and it limits your content, too. Why? Because in a world where every company is a publisher, you've got to cut through the din of mediocrity. You've got to experiment a little, be a little creative, and occasionally take risks.

- **Here's a good test:** Look at your content and ask yourself: Am I am taking any risks? Are you being creative enough? Are you showing your unique personality? Are you spending too much time trying to stay in the box instead of creating new levels in your industry?

Keep in mind that your content establishes you in the minds of your clients.

PAUSE. REVIEW. IMPLEMENT.

Content is where people learn from you and get a sense of your voice, and it is through your content they connect with you. I asked a couple of questions that I want to challenge you to address.
Are you taking any risks? Are you being creative enough? Are you showing your unique personality?

_____

_____

_____

_____

Will I Know Your Brand Tomorrow?

I am going to say something that will probably have some of you giving me the side eye or at least raise an eyebrow. Ok, here goes: I think the Kardashian family is a truly great example of how to keep your brand relevant. I am sure many of you will say that I could have come up with a better example, but let me share with you why I went with theirs, and how that can apply to us.

They are fully tapped into the interests of their audience. They have mastered the art of using social media in a way that makes their fans feel like they know them personally. By creating and establishing that relationship, their audience is more tuned into what they say, do, wear, who they are connected to, and where they go each day. Since their loyal audience feels like they know them, they support everything they do, design, create, and launch.

Ask Yourself:

How tuned into your audience are you? Do you really feel like they know you? Do you really know what your audience likes? What draws them in? What turns them away? What makes them feel valued? These are the questions I would challenge you to ask yourself. There is so much competing for the attention of your audience that if you are not fully tapped into them, their attention will go elsewhere. You don't want to be a one-hit wonder, right? So

They keep you guessing as to what they are going to do next. The media loves the Kardashians because they are consistently doing things that keeps their audience shocked, excited, guessing, happy, or upset. Regardless of what they do, they keep things fresh and different. Thus, they have remained relevant in their brand.

Ask Yourself:

Do you keep your audience excited about what you are going to do next? Do all your programs feel the same? Do you keep your content fresh and new? Is your approach to solutions dated, or is it current with the times?

One of the biggest mistakes an entrepreneur can make is to say, "I can't do that, because it won't work with my brand," or "We could never do that!" The truth is, your audience looks to you for creative solutions, out-of-the-box thinking, and fresh perspective on everyday challenges. So, I challenge you to keep an open mind when it comes to finding ways to maintain brand relevancy with your audience.

PAUSE. REVIEW. IMPLEMENT.

One challenge entrepreneurs face is staying current in their offerings and services. To keeping growing, you must have an engaged audience.

Do you keep your audience excited about what you are going to do next? Do all your programs feel the same? Is your approach to solutions dated, or is it with the times?

_____

_____

_____

Seven Critical Marketing Areas You Need to Have in Place to be Successful

There are seven critical areas in marketing every business must have in place. Think of this as your "Marketing Wheel." To make your business run smoother, be less stressful, less time-consuming, and excel faster, you must have all the spokes in place and balanced.

Through our members' generous sharing of their successes, we discovered that these extremely successful business owners each have seven critical marketing areas (i.e. spokes) in their wheels and consistently have them working at their maximum potential.

These seven critical areas are:

1. A market that is hungry to consume your message-and your product or service. (Too often, entrepreneurs build a business around no market.)

2. A marketing message that grabs your prospects' attention and gets them to read your marketing materials, blogs, sales letter, ads, and other related marketing pieces.

3. A system for increasing the lifetime customer value (LCV) of each customer, client, or patient. (This is not about getting a client, it's about retaining them!)

4. A system for reaching more customers who don't make purchasing decisions based on price.

5. A lead-generating machine that never leaves you wondering where your next customer, client, or patient is coming from.

6. Offline strategies for getting your marketing message in front of your customers.

7. Online strategies for siphoning more leads and sales to your business.

Take a minute to honestly rate yourself on each of the spokes of your marketing wheel-from "1" being non-existent to "10" being outstanding. For example, if you don't have a system for reaching customers (who don't focus on cost but rather value), then you would rate yourself a 1; or if you have tried reaching out to this market, but don't have a system that consistently works, then you might rate yourself a 5.

This will not only help you determine where you are weakest and can improve the most, but it will also show you whether you are balanced. For instance, if you rate yourself a 10 on offline strategies, but a 1 on online strategies, you can't experience a thriving business.

Make each of your "spokes" strong, and you will have a business that provides you with the income that allows you to take vacations without feeling guilty, one you look forward to going to each day without having worries constantly keeping you awake at night.

PAUSE. REVIEW. IMPLEMENT.

In an age where technology is progressing rapidly, it is easy to forget one of the critical areas I mentioned: offline marketing strategies.

What can you do to improve your offline strategies for getting your marketing message in front of your customers?

_____

_____

_____

_____

Would You Work with Yourself?

I know that is an odd question, but it is so relevant to being successful.

How so?

I have shared often that "what you put out there, you will get back." If you are looking for clients to make resolute decisions about working with you and not "price shop" for a lengthy period, ask yourself whether you do the same thing to others.

If you have ever worked in a corporate environment, you may have heard of the 360 Degree evaluation. This is where your peers, supervisor, and anyone else who works directly with you are asked to give an honest assessment about what it is like to work with you. It can be brutal, but it is so necessary to really grow personally and professionally.

The same goes for being in business. An as entrepreneur, you need to know whether you are someone who a potential client would want to work with. Maybe you have clients leaving or not renewing with you. If you are struggling with finding new business, converting clients, closing those sales conversations, getting clients to pay on time, positioning your brand, etc., then look at the questions below. See if any of them resonate with you.

Ask yourself these questions:

- Do you make resolute decisions?
- Are you on time and prepared for meetings on a consistent basis?
- Do you invest in your own entrepreneurial development?
- Do you handle change well?
- Do you honor your financial commitments?
- Do you seek to support those around you?
- Can people trust what you say you are going to do?
- Do you send referrals to those you know in business?
- Are you teachable, or open to learn new things?
- Do you handle conflict or tough situations well?
- Do you make commitments, and then break them?
- To go one step further: Do you break commitments and choose not to tell the person you are not moving forward with him/her?
- When people email you, do you answer their emails in a timely fashion, or ignore them?
- When people ask you for a testimonial/feedback, do you provide one if you enjoyed the service, program, or event?
- Do you give extra value (over deliver/under promise) to your clients/customers?
- Do you communicate well with those you work and/or partner with?
- Do you keep healthy boundaries with clients/customers?
- Do you balance your priorities with family and your business?
- Do you create an environment that enables a new client/customer to feel comfortable working with you?

- Are you approachable, friendly, and inviting?

The list can go on and on. Give yourself a 360 Degree evaluation, and ask some of your clients (past and present) to provide feedback. You want to be someone whom your current and potential clients feel they know, like, and trust.

PAUSE. REVIEW. IMPLEMENT.

One of the hardest things we can do is be honest with ourselves. Sometimes our marketing, products, services, or even our branding isn't helping. I listed several questions that you can ask yourself. I challenge you to answer at least five of them.

_____

_____

_____

_____

Make generosity part of
your growth strategy.

Brand Trust: Does Your Audience Trust You?

Think about that one person you call your true friend, that person who is there for you no matter what. I would venture to guess that you built this trust over time by seeing how they interacted with you, how they kept their word, how they treated you, and how they added to your life. Next, I would venture to guess that if they made a mistake, you would forgive them, because you know that that mistake is not indicative of who they are. Now, think about this in relation to your brand.

Consistency: Like any relationship, trust is built over time. So, ask yourself the following questions:

- **How consistent am I being in my level of engagement?**

  When I consider engagement, I immediately think about ballroom dancing. You must trust the person you are dancing with from start to finish. The same goes with building trust in your business. From the time you court your prospective client to the time their season with you is over, you should strive for consistency in how you engage with them. Typically, in the beginning, it is like a honeymoon where everything is exciting in that working relationship. However, it is important that you continue to engage your clients. That builds trust in you, and it prompts them to share their level of trust in you with others.

- **How consistent am I being in my messaging?**

  Does what you say you do match up to what your audience reads on your website, in blogs, on your posts, and in your business conversations? If your messaging is not aligned, you will find that potential clients will have a hard time joining your programs, trusting your expertise, and they will usually not return to learn more about you.

- **How consistent am I being in what I say?**

  This is rooted in how you keep your word. For example, if you say that you publish a bi-weekly newsletter, then make sure it comes out every two weeks. Sounds simple, right? Not being consistent in the integrity of what you say you will do can cause mistrust.

So, consider how consistent you are, and whether you are building brand trust.

PAUSE. REVIEW. IMPLEMENT.

When it comes to business, trust is everything. If your audience and clients don't trust you, they won't work with you or buy from you.

How consistent are you being in your level of engagement?

How consistent are you being in your messaging?

How consistent are you being in what you say?

_____

_____

_____

My Final Thoughts

There are many decisions that you must make as a business owner that matters. These decisions need to feel good to you and reflect what your values are. Anytime a decision you make costs you your peace, it is not worth the cost.

Here are a few decisions that matter:

- ❖ How you engage with your team, clients, and vendors
- ❖ The quality of the content that you create and share
- ❖ Taking time to pause and really reflect on what is going on around you and in your business
- ❖ The environment that you are building within
- ❖ How you develop your clients' experience with you
- ❖ How you define the value that you offer
- ❖ What you choose to accept and reject
- ❖ How you enhance your knowledge
- ❖ The conversations you have with yourself
- ❖ How you view yourself as a business owner

My hope and prayer is that you were able to gain at least one nugget that you can put in place to further your growth as a business owner. Whatever you have gained, commit to putting action behind your decisions.

It Matters:
Decisions That Will Make or Break Your Business

There are many things in business that matter. These things affect whether you grow or stay stagnant, and whether you increase or decrease your clientele. Simply put, there are things that determine whether you will stay in business or go out of business.

There are things that matter that often are overlooked, ignored, brushed over, or tried once-but because the desired results did not happen they are never looked at again. So, I wanted to walk through several areas that I personally feel matter when it comes to developing a sustainable and profitable business.

A Few Amazon Reviews:

"*It Matters* is a raw, honest, and relevant book that addresses some of life's curveballs that sometimes affects a business mindset. As I read this book, I quickly realized that it will become a relevant guide that I will refer to time and time again. The lessons embedded caused me to be reflective of my own practices, thoughts, attitudes and words. *It Matters* takes your thinking a step further with a section that literally makes you pause and think about the different lessons/truths, how these apply to you and your business, and of course, how to leverage those to maximize your growth! *It Matters* is a great resource to add to your library!"

"*It Matters* is high on the list of books that I wish I had read when I started my business. However, after being in business now more than fifteen years, it truly gave me so many great points to pause, examine, and review. That is what I enjoyed the most. I like to read books that challenge me in how I see my systems and processes. *It Matters* delivers on all fronts. One thing I loved about the book is that Kimberly has written the content in a way that inspires and challenges you, and she poses the information in a way that [will have] you look at your business in a fresh way. More importantly, she talks about the areas of business that honestly matter. That is what drew me to the book. Great read!"

"I have enjoyed reading this book. Especially the chapter on being resolved. The tips and the take away are very good information for entrepreneurs to use in their journeys. Many of the stories that she highlights resonate so well with me and my journey, and I am sure that others will find things in these passages that can be used as helpful information for them. This book truly mattered to me, and I am certain that it will matter to you. A truly great read."

"*It Matters* captivates the true spirit of the entrepreneur by connecting what we want to happen with what we need to do to make it happen. The book is simple to read, yet inspiring with personal stories that paint a picture and drive a point. It allows the reader to absorb the subject matter, evaluate it personally, and then it challenges you to act. Kimberly's advice is timeless and necessary!"

ABOUT
KIMBERLY DESHIELDS-SPENCER

Kimberly DeShields-Spencer won't tell you that she created and ran a successful lemonade stand when she was seven years old. Even then, she knew how to take the lemons in her life and make...money. She has spent over two decades cultivating her particular brand of expertise, earning two master's and a bachelor's degree in business administration and organizational development along the way. But she won't tell you that. Why? Because for her, the proof is in the pudding. Kimberly doesn't care about accolades or awards. She cares about people-and the results that she can help them garner by creating individualized and effective action plans to accomplish their goals.

Kimberly has been featured on and in numerous magazines and has served on a variety of boards (that she won't allow to be listed here) as she's blazed a trail of care, creativity, and community throughout her career. She has taken her considerable experience and synthesized it into several best-selling books, such as It Matters: Decisions that will Make or Break Your Business. She hosts a successful podcast that boasts up to 5,000 downloads a month. And that's not all...

She is a mogul-in-the-making, having founded UImpact, UImpact Publishing Group, Behind Her Brand, She Can Academy, and The DeShields Foundation along with her sons, Christian and Cayden.

But again, none of these things are what she wants people to focus on when it comes to her. So why list them? Because it's important to point out how her laser focus on what really matters translates to her achieving more than just what she sets out to. And this is worth noting because it is a blueprint for business people to consider when they want to learn to strive for more. In short, Kimberly DeShields-Spencer has developed a knack for having her cake and eating it, too. And the best part is, she loves to teach others to do the same.

Kimberly won't tell anyone to walk across hot coals. She won't glide into a meeting with roller blades on. She won't dance a beat with her clients. But she will push them off a ledge. Not literally, of course, but she will do what it takes to teach them to fly. She blends a no-nonsense, direct delivery with disarming warmth, concern, and personal attention. But most importantly, she doesn't just make an impact, she leaves one. The difference? She isn't content with just affecting immediate change, so Kimberly instills in people how to keep pumping their wells. For good.

As she continues to build with her dedicated team of passionate men and women, Kimberly's star is steadily rising. A stalwart of radiant confidence that everyone can be so much more than they allow themselves to.

To connect with Kimberly:

Website:
www.uimpact.net

LinkedIn:
www.linkedin.com/in/uimpact

Instagram:
@KimberlyUImpact

www.ingramcontent.com/pod-product-compliance
Lightning Source LLC
Chambersburg PA
CBHW052319220526
45472CB00001B/190